Gillen.

This booklet was written by Rory Gillen, founder of GillenMarkets, and is also available in eBook format (PDF, ePub or Kindle).

About Gillen

Gillen is a boutique investment advisor offering expert advice on the management of personal, pension and corporate monies. We place a strong emphasis on fully understanding our clients' needs, so that we can make informed decisions and plans, together.

We are investment advisors, not product sellers. Our investment solutions are structured to meet the specific needs of each individual client with minimum assets of €500k.

Our investment advisory fee structure aligns our interests with yours, ensuring that we sit on the same side of the table as our clients.

With our fee structure, there are:

- No upfront commissions or fees payable by clients.
- No dealing costs.
- No early redemption penalties.
- No VAT.

Just a transparent 1.0% annual advisory fee on the assets under advice.

We also offer a subscription-based investment newsletter for do-it-yourself investors and training courses both in-person and online for those wishing to learn more about the principles of sound investing.

We believe trust is earned. Our belief is that we work for clients, looking at each individual's needs and taking a commonsense, long-term approach.

We have built an outstanding team with the depth of knowledge and experience to meet all our clients' investment needs. We have an appetite for learning and sharing and we always partner with our clients as equals.

We'd like to hear from you!

Contact details

T: + 353 (0)1 287 1400
E: info@gillenmarkets.com
W: www.gillenmarkets.com

Follow us on Facebook, LinkedIn, Twitter and Gillenmarkets.com.

ILTB Ltd (trading as Gillen/GillenMarkets) is regulated by the Central Bank of Ireland.

A Path to Financial Freedom

A Guide to Sound Investing

(2nd edition / 2023)

A **GillenMarkets** Publication

Rory Gillen

Published by OAK TREE PRESS, Cork T12 XY2N
www.oaktreepress.com / www.SuccessStore.com

© 2023 ILTB Ltd t/a GillenMarkets

A catalogue record of this book is available from the British Library.

ISBN 978 1 78119 575 6 (Paperback)
ISBN 978 1 78119 576 5 (PDF)
ISBN 978 1 78119 577 2 (ePub)
ISBN 978 1 78119 578 9 (Kindle)

Disclaimer
Investing carries risk and none of the stocks or funds highlighted in this booklet constitute a recommendation by the author, GillenMarkets or the publisher and none of these parties can assume liability for any losses that may be sustained should a reader subsequently invest in them, and any such liability is hereby disclaimed. Readers should take professional advice before making any investment. None of the material in this publication constitutes investment advice or an offer to invest in any of the funds referred to. No one receiving this publication should treat it as a personal recommendation as it does not take into account the needs and objectives, personal circumstances, including investment experience, financial position, or attitude to risk of recipients.
Warning
Past performance is not a reliable guide to future performance.

CONTENTS

Gillen.

Other Publications from GillenMarkets

3 STEPS TO INVESTMENT SUCCESS (2012)
How to Obtain the Returns While Controlling the Risk
Rory Gillen

TIMING THE MARKETS (2023)
Unemotional Approaches to Making Buy & Sell Decisions in Markets
Rory Gillen

BRICKS & MORTAR THROUGH STOCKS & SHARES (2023)
Property Investing in the Stock Markets
Darren Gillen

PRIVATE EQUITY: ACCESS FOR ALL (2023)
Investing in Private Equity through the Stock Markets
Jonathan Yates

INTELLIGENT GOLD INVESTING (2nd edition / 2023)
Including a Section on Bitcoin
Rory Gillen

UNDERSTANDING ALTERNATIVE ASSETS (2nd edition / 2023)
Gold, Forestry, Government & Corporate Bonds, Renewable Energy & Hedge Strategies
Rory Gillen

All available in print and ebook formats from
GillenMarkets.com, SuccessStore.com & Amazon

FOREWORD

As one who believes passionately in encouraging and educating the private investor, I have long felt that there was a big gap in the market for very 'easy-to-read' booklets rather than the heavier tomes of which there are a substantial number. *A Guide to Sound Investing* by Rory Gillen is just the sort of publication I have had in mind, and it covers most of the investment basics in an easily readable and digestible way. While obviously written with the Irish investor in mind, its fundamental messages have wider appeal and it is well worth reading by the novice investor, particularly from the younger generation.

Lord John Lee
Financial Times **columnist and Liberal Democrat Peer**

INTRODUCTION

Learning how to save and invest is not a luxury, it is a crucial part of our lives, and we need to be more informed. The disaster that was wreaked on people's savings and investments (and lives) in Ireland in particular following the Irish banking and fiscal crises in 2008, and the personal traumas inflicted, need not have happened if people had understood how to invest. That we learn little about even the basics of saving and investing in school or university is part of the problem.

For decades, employers in both the private and public sectors were willing to accept the risks that go with funding employees' pensions. In the private sector, this is no longer the case; increasingly, people have to look out for their own retirement income.

This booklet on saving and investing should be relevant to a significant and growing proportion of society. But even those with a guaranteed pension income in retirement, from their employer or the State, can benefit from the messages in this booklet about how to achieve financial freedom – and much earlier in life than you might previously have thought.

Over a normal lifetime, while bank deposits and government bonds have traditionally provided safe avenues for savings, the best returns have always come from investing in businesses or property. The simple fact is that returns from business and property are typically much higher than bank deposit returns over the medium- to long-term. And it can be remarkably easy to invest in real businesses and property using the stock markets (or life assurance companies), if you keep things simple. Keeping things simple, of course, requires would-be investors to gain a basic understanding of investing, the choice of assets available and the risks that need to be avoided. This booklet on saving and investing aims to assist you to do just that.

A fundamental truth in investing is that you must own an asset if you want the returns from it. Owning shares gives you part-ownership of businesses, and that can be empowering. Invest in markets as you would in a private property: by owning a house or an apartment, you benefit from the natural rise in property prices over time as their values adjust higher to reflect the growth in personal incomes in a prospering economy. And so it is with business, and businesses listed on the stock markets. As economies grow, companies' earnings grow, and for companies traded on stock markets as a group their share prices follow the upward growth in their earnings over time.

Of course, share prices of businesses and property companies or Real Estate Investment Trusts (REITs) listed on stock markets never advance in a straight line, and their long-term uptrends are often interrupted by economic downturns or negative political developments. And property or share prices that get overvalued compared with their underlying fundamentals (incomes or earnings) are susceptible to more serious corrections. The overvaluation of Irish property in the 2003 to 2007 period and subsequent 50% decline in prices from 2008 to 2012 is a case in point.

Would-be investors also need an understanding of the difference between investing in markets and trading markets. To trade markets – trying to buy low and sell high over short time intervals – is akin to speculating; and, if you speculate in markets, you are likely to sooner or later get the same results as you would down in the bookies.

Trying to avoid the risks inherent in owning property or shares by, for example, choosing a fund with a guarantee is not the answer either. If only it was that easy! Like many areas in life, there's no free lunch. If you want the higher returns that the stock markets or physical property deliver over time, you must take the risk that comes with owning these assets. Good investing is learning how to mitigate those risks.

The property and banking bust in Ireland in 2008 surely taught us all that using debt to try and finance an asset or boost returns adds risk. Using debt potentially adds a lot of risk if you buy overvalued assets. In Ireland, for those who prefer investing in property, the life companies offer property funds without any debt and there is a plethora of good quality REITs listed on the Irish, UK and European stock exchanges. The life companies and stock market-listed property REITs give you diversified exposure to office, retail, industrial and residential property. The proposition of buying good quality property assets (*via* REITs or life company funds) bit by bit over time should be more attractive to many savers starting out than having to buy a single physical property at a point in time, and often having to finance it with debt. In other words, using the stock markets and life companies to invest in property is easy, carries less risk, and the choice available on stock markets is greater.

For younger savers and those saving through a pension, who can invest regularly, in up markets and down markets, the risks of mistiming your entry into markets and getting poor value – which can reduce the subsequent returns – are hugely mitigated when you are investing consistently over time.

Forget about the political and economic news flow of the day. Recognise that you can't see the future – nor can anyone else for that matter. It is another fundamental principle of investing that you do not need to predict the future in order to make a success out of investing.

What you do need is a basic understanding of investing and the risks you are taking, and a glass-half-full attitude. Economies have made continuous upward progress over time (in the developed world at least) such that it generally pays to have an optimistic outlook. Living standards today are probably some four to five times higher than for the average person in Ireland even just one generation ago.

One important aim of this booklet is to provide you with a common-sense understanding of the key risks you face as an investor. If you can't identify what the risks are at the outset, then it's going to be pretty hard for you to avoid them.

We intuitively know that driving a car can be dangerous. The risks (of accidents) are high if the basic rules are not adhered to. These rules include learning how to drive, driving slowly in congested areas, ensuring the car is in good working order, paying attention to road signs, and many other rules that act to safeguard against the risks. By controlling the risks of driving in this way, the majority of drivers get to enjoy the enormous benefits of driving while avoiding the risks. But there can be no guarantee that you'll never have an accident, and the parallels with investing are striking. The benefits of investing in risk assets – like property or businesses listed on the stock markets – are the potentially higher returns, but we must control the risks.

You cannot invest without savings. So, start a savings plan before you even consider buying a house to live in. If you can't save 10% before all else, then you are in danger of always having to work for money. If you can build an asset base from which you can earn an independent income, you can achieve financial freedom – and much earlier in life than you may think. You can't eat the house you live in, so your home is not an asset. It's a lifestyle!

Lastly, the Internet has substantially lowered the costs of transacting in stock markets with the advent of online stockbroking accounts in the mid- to late-1990s. Today, the informed investor can put her savings to work at substantially lower cost than was possible before the Internet. And the costs of investing through the stock markets are a fraction of the costs involved in physical property investing.

1: WHY STOCK MARKETS GENERATE HIGHER RETURNS

A reasonable question to ask is: Why have shares (stock markets) and physical property delivered better returns than bank deposits over time?

From the dawn of time, people have always traded with each other. From trade and specialisation, businesses develop, which leads to growth in the economy. If the returns generated by businesses, in aggregate, were not higher than what could be earned from bank deposits, why would a businessperson take the risk of putting capital into her own business? If bank deposit returns were higher than could be earned in business – where there is risk – we would all be better off leaving our savings sitting idle in the bank. If everyone did this, of course, there would be no investing – only saving – and interest rates would decline to zero as there would be no demand for money (credit).

Table 1.1: After-tax Returns on Net Capital Employed

Company	Financial Year	After-tax Profits (m)	Shareholders' Funds (m)	Return on Equity
Coca-Cola	Dec-21	9,771	21,149	46.2%
DCC	Mar-22	424	2,776	15.3%
Grafton	Dec-21	222	1,593	14.0%
Heineken	Dec-21	3,324	15,374	21.6%
Kerry Group	Dec-21	675	5,129	13.2%
Reckitts	Dec-21	2,053	8,257	24.9%
Mincon	Dec-21	15	139	10.5%
Average		**16,485**	**54,416**	**20.8%**

Source: Companies' Annual Reports.

Table 1.1 outlines the after-tax earnings and net capital employed (shareholders' funds) for seven businesses – including such well-known international companies as Coca-Cola, Heineken and Reckitts and a selection of Irish companies: DCC, Grafton, Kerry and Mincon. The returns these companies made in their respective financial year on the net capital employed in their businesses ranged from 46.2% for Coca-Cola to 10.5% for Mincon, the Shannon-based mining engineering company. The average return on equity[1] (net capital employed) for the seven companies is 20.8%. That's well ahead of what one can earn on bank deposits.

Of course, most of the time you can't purchase these businesses at their balance sheet values (net capital employed) in the marketplace. Because these businesses, and most businesses, earn returns that are well in excess of bank deposit returns, investors pay a premium valuation for these businesses.

Table 1.2: The Earnings Yield

	After-tax Profits (m)	Shareholders' Funds (m)	Return on Equity	Market Value (m) 29-Oct-22	Earnings Yield 29-Oct-22
Coca-Cola	9,771	21,149	46.2%	259,647	3.8%
DCC	424	2,776	15.3%	4,779	8.9%
Grafton	222	1,593	14.0%	1,586	14.0%
Heineken	3,324	15,374	21.6%	48,431	6.9%
Kerry Group	675	5,129	13.2%	15,917	4.2%
Reckitts	2,053	8,257	24.9%	40,558	5.1%
Mincon	15	139	10.5%	213	6.9%
Average	**16,485**	**54,416**	**20.8%**	**371,131**	**7.1%**

Source: Companies' Annual Reports & Bloomberg.

Table 1.2 highlights that in contrast to the value of shareholders' funds, the value investors attribute to these same companies is a lot higher. For example, Heineken's shareholders' funds was €15,374 million but the value investors were putting on the company at 29th October 2022 was €48,431 million. So, while Heineken was generating a 21.6% return on equity (or on its

---

[1]   Represents the simple average of the returns on equity of the seven companies.

shareholders' funds), an investor buying the shares on 29th October 2022 was getting a lower earnings yield of 6.9%. And the simple average earnings yield to an investor who bought all seven shares in **Table 1.2** on that same day was 7.1%, in contrast to the average return on equity for these companies of 20.8%.

But that initial 7.1% earnings yield (similar to the rental yield on a property) was a lot higher than the investor could have earned from bank deposits back in late October 2022. Even at the date of writing this booklet, bank deposit rates in the developed world remain below 5.0%. And one might reasonably expect these companies to grow their earnings over time, so that the earnings yield can also grow over time. This is why investors are prepared to pay a premium, often a large premium, over balance sheet value for companies listed on the stock markets.

As stock markets are just a collection of publicly listed businesses, it follows that stock market returns tend to be higher than bank deposit rates over the long-term.

Of course, the underlying assumption an investor makes is that she is dealing with a market where democracy is the order of the day, and where the government is pro-business. Markets in more politically unstable areas of the world have not necessarily delivered returns greater than risk-free bank deposits. But then, in such countries, even bank deposits are rarely risk-free. Think Russia, Venezuela, Argentina, Turkey, Syria, Afghanistan to name but a few!

The progress of the stock markets is tracked through stock market indices. In the US, the S&P 500 Index was introduced in the 1950s to track the performance of 500 leading US companies across a range of industries; the index is also used to reflect the performance of the broader US economy. In Ireland, we have the ISEQ Overall Index, which tracks the average performance of all the companies listed on the Irish Stock Exchange. And there are also 'World Equity' indices, such as the MSCI World Index or the FTSE World Index, which track the performance of a large selection of companies from many different countries in order to provide a guide to the progress of the global stock markets.

In order to provide some facts to back up the claim that stock markets produce better returns than bank deposits over time, we will turn to the S&P 500 Index.

Chart 1.1: S&P 500 Earnings per share (1950 to 2022)

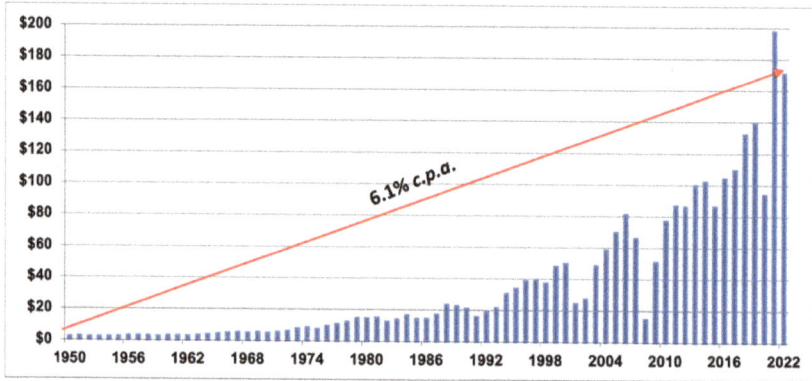

Source: S&P Dow Jones Indices.

Chart 1.1 highlights the aggregate annual earnings of the 500 companies making up the S&P 500 Index from 1950 to 2022 inclusive. Just as one can add up all the share prices of these 500 leading companies to get a single index value (the S&P 500 Index value), so too can we add up all the earnings of these 500 companies and get a single earnings value.

Chart 1.1 highlights that the 500 companies making up the S&P 500 Index earned $2.32 per index share at the end of 1949. At the time of writing, earnings for the current 500 companies in the S&P 500 Index are expected to be $171.34 per share for 2022. Over this 73-year period from 1950 to 2022 inclusive, earnings for the S&P 500 Index have grown at a rate of 6.1% compound *per annum*.

As **Table 1.3** highlights, over the same timeline the S&P 500 Index itself rose from 16.84 at the start of 1950 to 3,839 by end December 2022 for growth of 7.7% compound *per annum*.

Share prices follow earnings over the long-term. However, over the 73-year period from 1950 to 2022 inclusive, the capital returns from the S&P 500 Index were 1.6% *per annum* higher than the growth in the S&P 500 Index earnings.

In late 1949, investors were prepared to pay only 7.3 times the earnings of the index ($2.32 * 7.3 = 16.84). By end 2022, investors were paying 22.4 times the S&P 500 Index earnings. This higher multiple that investors were prepared to pay for earnings by end 2022 compared to what they were prepared to pay in late 1949 accounts for the extra 1.6% *per annum* returns.

For you, the investor in shares in that index, individually or *via* a fund, your capital grew at that same rate, 7.7% annually (less costs).

Table 1.3: S&P 500 Index – Price and Dividend Returns

	S&P 500 Index
1 January 1950	17
31 December 2022	3,839
Annual Growth	7.7%
Average Dividend Yield	3.1%
Total Annual Return	**10.8%**

Source: S&P Dow Jones Indices and Bloomberg.

In addition, the average annual dividend paid by the 500 companies making up the S&P 500 Index over this 73-year timeline from the start of 1950 to end 2022 was 3.1%. Investors received this dividend stream in cash. In total, then, investors' capital grew at 7.7% annually and they also on average received 3.1% annually by way of dividends for total annual returns of 10.8%. You might put the annual costs of owning shares or a fund invested in the S&P 500 Index at 0.5% *per annum,* so that net returns might have been in the order of 10.3% annually. For the sake of simplicity, we ignore taxes.

Over the same timeline, returns from US short-term bank deposits averaged 4.3% compound *per annum.*[2] So, for taking the risk, US equities provided a 6.5% premium return annually (or 6.0% after assumed costs) since the start of 1950. This is referred to in the industry as the 'risk premium', or the premium return over bank deposits for taking the risk.

Thus, we have shown that the US stock market provided returns well in excess of bank deposits over this 73-year timeline. There are many formal studies available to prove that the same holds true for other developed stock markets like Ireland, the UK, Europe and Asia. The availability of higher returns

---

[2]   *Barclays Equity Gilt Study*, 2022.

from the stock markets is, of course, the reason to consider saving and investing through the stock markets.

We also must understand that the upward march of business and the stock markets is often interrupted. The business cycle is alive and well and economic progress is often punctuated by recessions that lead to downturns in business. Such downturns result in lower business earnings and, in the stock markets, lower share prices. As we don't know, and can't see, the future, an essential part of successful investing is having the belief that markets will recover after setbacks.

As **Chart 1.1** highlights, earnings at the 500 companies making up the S&P 500 Index declined on several occasions over the period in question. The oil price-driven recession of the mid-1970s saw earnings decline 10% between 1974 and 1975. Earnings declined again by 18% in 1982 during the recession that occurred when the Federal Reserve (the US Central Bank) hiked interest rates in order to cool the high inflation that prevailed at that time. Earnings declined again in 1991, by 25%, in response to the Gulf war. Once again, following the bursting of the global tech bubble in early 2000, earnings declined by 45% in 2001 before recovering sharply thereafter. Earnings collapsed 81% following the Global Financial Crisis from 2007 to 2009, only to rebound to a new earnings peak by 2011. The Covid-19 pandemic saw earnings on the S&P 500 Index decline by 33% in 2020 before recovering to a new earnings peak in 2021, as the US government spent freely to underpin wages and demand in the US economy generally.

Stock markets are volatile because the business cycle is not smooth and is often interrupted by recessions caused by a variety of factors. This volatility is then amplified by investors over-reacting relative to the underlying decline in earnings. However, as the march of economies and business is ever upwards, stock markets tend to recover from these setbacks, so that this volatility is not something to fear. In fact, such setbacks offer up lower prices and better values, which improve the subsequent returns for investors who buy during such declines.

2: SAVE 10% OF YOUR INCOME BEFORE ALL ELSE

In a remarkably simple and entertaining book, **The Richest Man in Babylon**,[3] author George S. Clason communicates the core messages of saving and investing through fictional financial parables set in ancient Babylon. The characters throughout the book are typically traders and merchants – self-made men – who live in the Mesopotamian city of Babylon and who explain the secrets of their wealth to poorer men and slaves who wish to better their lot in life.

The city of Babylon was famed in its time as a jewel of the Mesopotamian Empire. It was a city with very few natural resources surrounded by an arid valley; and yet, as a result of human innovation and ingenuity, the city thrived as a commercial and cultural hub in its time. It is no accident, then, that the book is set here: the author views the city as an "outstanding example of man's ability to achieve great objectives, using whatever means are at his disposal". All of Babylon's riches were man-made.

In Chapter 3 of the book, King Sargon returns from a war and laments the poor state into which his city has fallen. Prior to the war, he had initiated a series of public works (infrastructure projects) which brought wealth to all its citizens; however, in the time since the works have been completed, all of the wealth created has ended up in the hands of a few rich men such that the gap between poor and rich has become intolerably wide.

---

[3] From *The Richest Man in Babylon* by George S. Clason, copyright 1926, 1930-33, 1936-37, 1940, 1946-47, 1954-55 by George S. Clason; copyright renewed © 1983 by Clyde Clason. Used by permission of Dutton, an imprint of Penguin Publishing Group, a division of Penguin Random House LLC.

The King's chancellor warns the King that "one may not condemn a man for succeeding because he knows how. Neither may one with justice take away from a man what he has fairly earned, to give to men of less ability".

Discarding, then, the idea of wealth redistribution as a solution, the King summons Arkad, the richest man in Babylon, and confers with him. The King asks Arkad to lecture at a school for teachers, that each teacher might be trained in the ways of finance and then spread these teachings across the city. In this way, the citizens of Babylon could learn to make themselves wealthy and thus reduce the city's wealth inequality.

Before a seminar of 100 men, Arkad divulged the seven secrets of wealth that he had learned from a lifetime of saving:

- **'Start Thy Purse to Fattening:** For every 10 coins you place within your purse, take out for use but nine.' *Comment:* Save 10% of your income before all else. If you cannot save from your earnings, you cannot start to grow an asset base and 10% seems a reasonable objective.

- **'Control Thy Expenditures: Budget your expenses that you may have coins to pay for your necessities, to pay for your enjoyments and to gratify your worthwhile desires without spending more than nine-tenths of your earnings.'** *Comment:* If you first set aside 10% of your income before all else, you will find it easier to confine your outlays to the remaining 90%. In other words, saving is a habit, and it becomes easier the more you practice it. Like the merchants and slaves in Babylon, it is surprising how easy it becomes to keep your outgoings to 90% of your earnings when you make that a key objective.

- **'Make Thy Gold Multiply: To put each coin to labouring that it may reproduce its kind even as the flocks of the field and help bring to thee income, a stream of wealth that shall flow constantly into your purse.'** *Comment:* Invest your savings and reinvest the income from your investments and watch your assets grow. This is the basic law of compounding. In Babylonian times, gold, silver and property were the principal assets; today, there's a greater variety of assets in which to invest your savings – from bank deposits to government and corporate bonds to precious metals, from property to equities: the choices abound.

- **'Guard Thy Treasures from Loss: To invest only where your principal is safe, where it may be reclaimed if desirable, and where you will not fail to collect a fair rental. Consult with wise men. Secure the advice of those experienced in the profitable handling of gold. Let their wisdom protect your treasure from unsafe investments.'** *Comment:* Learn how to invest and to control what the risks involved. Few in Irish society understood risk during the property boom; it should humble us as a society that the Babylonians understood these simple principles over 5,000 years ago, and George S. Clason over 100 years ago. Why is it that each generation learns from the previous one in matters of law, science, the arts and medicine, but not in matters of money?

- **'Make of Thy Dwelling a Profitable Investment.'** *Comment:* Yes, we understand this one in Ireland! But the desire to own a home should come after a savings programme, not before. It's no coincidence that Arkad placed this secret at number 5 on his list, and not number 1. His message was: save 10% of your earnings before all else, and then consider buying your home to improve your security and quality of life.

- **'Insure a Future Income: Provide in advance for the needs of your growing age and the protection of your family.'** *Comment:* Consider life and income insurance for the times when you won't be able to earn as much as before, or to provide for your family in case the Lord calls you earlier than expected.

- **'Increase Thy Ability to Earn: To cultivate your own powers, to study and become wiser, to become more skilful, to so act as to respect yourself.'** *Comment:* Gain greater skills, so that you can increase your earning power.

It is the first rule – that investors should set aside 10% of their income – which is the most important. This rule supersedes all other rules; it is a prerequisite to financial success and forms the cornerstone of any good savings programme. For example, rule number 5 states that people should own their own home – but this means being able to afford the mortgage after you have already saved 10% of your income, not before!

You might ask, what difference can saving just 10% of your income make? As we shall see in **Chapter 3: THE REMARKABLE POWER OF COMPOUNDING**, the answer is: a surprisingly large amount, if you start early.

To save a lump-sum of capital from which you can earn an income that covers your annual outgoings is to achieve financial freedom. More people in society can achieve this, and earlier than you might think, but it takes a plan and discipline to achieve it.

Of course, not everyone in society is driven to acquire assets or to achieve financial freedom within their own lifetime. There is, as they say, more to life than money – and quite right, too! Nonetheless, if you want financial freedom in your own lifetime, Clason's basic rules for acquiring it ring as true today as they did when he wrote them, and as true as they did back in Babylonian times.

3: THE REMARKABLE POWER OF COMPOUNDING

You cannot compound from zero, so you need to start somewhere and then have some patience; compounding works wonders given time. Compounding is not as important to those who already have a lump-sum to invest, be that from the sale of a business, from the inheritance of a property or simply from having saved *via* a pension plan. This chapter, then, is aimed more towards the person starting without a significant, or indeed any, capital base.

The success of your investment programme depends on a couple of key variables:

- The amount of money you commit;
- The rate of return you achieve;
- The length of time you commit to saving and investing; and
- The tax efficiency of your savings programme.

STARTING A SAVINGS PROGRAMME

As we saw in **Chapter 1: WHY STOCK MARKETS GENERATE HIGHER RETURNS**, US equities have delivered *circa* 6.0% after costs annually more than bank deposits over the decades. For many years following the Global Financial Crisis, bank deposit rates had been close to zero and even negative for a while. However, in the US and Eurozone they started to rise in early 2022. For the sake of forecasting, then, we might assume that bank deposit rates in the Eurozone will average 3% annually from here. Global Equities are more expensive today compared to the early 1950s, so that we will assume annual returns of 7.0% going forward.

Chapter 2: SAVE 10% OF YOUR INCOME BEFORE ALL ELSE suggests that you save 10% of your income. According to the Central Statistics Office (CSO), at the time of writing the average gross income of those employed in Ireland was recorded at €45,900. Under current pension rules, you get tax relief on contributions you make to a pension scheme, and so we will assume that you save €4,590 (10%) into a pension account annually. If we further assume that your employer makes a 5% annual contribution to your pension of €2,295, then you can actually save €6,885 annually into your pension savings programme based on just your own 10% contribution (see **Table 3.1**). That's a savings programme the average person in society can manage.

Table 3.1: Average Gross Income[4] and Contribution to a Pension Fund

	€
Average Gross Income of those Employed	45,900
Save 10% of Gross Income to Pension	4,590
Employer Contribution (5% assumed)	2,295
Gross Contribution to Pension	**€6,885**
Saving 10% from After-tax Income	€3,600

Source: Central Statistics Office & GillenMarkets' assumptions.

Table 3.1 also highlights what a significant difference it makes saving through a pension vehicle. Saving 10% from your after-tax income would probably mean you could save just €3,600 annually, almost half of what you can do using the pension structure.

We will address this chapter to the person joining the workforce who can probably start saving from, say, age 26 onwards. This means a 40-year savings programme until retirement at the current normal age of 65: today, with improving healthcare and longer lifespans, many people can expect to live many years beyond this milestone. For those who have built up some savings,

---

[4]   The personal income figure in **Table 3.1** is derived from CSO data, which showed that average weekly earnings in Ireland (seasonally adjusted) were €897.41 for the fourth quarter of 2022, or €46,665 annualised. Deriving an average earnings number from the national accounts and labour statistics gives a higher average annual income of €57,900 per person employed, and includes other items such as bonuses, earnings, and commissions. **Table 3.1** has taken its lead from the CSO numbers and should be considered theoretical.

they are in the enviable position of being able to choose what they would like to do in their golden years – whether that is to retire, to tour the world, or to pursue some other activity that interests them. For others, it may be about having the flexibility to retire early. In that case, they may have to contribute more to any savings plan they establish in order to get to a target lump-sum that can deliver an income that will cover their annual costs in retirement.

THE RATE OF RETURN MATTERS

Table 3.2 shows the value of a €6,885 annual pension savings programme started at age 26 that invests in risk-free bank deposits and obtains a 3% annual return and compares it with the alternative of investing in risk assets *via* a global equity fund and obtaining an annual 7% return. It is unlikely that the average income in society as outlined in the CSO statistics is representative of what the average person aged 26 will be earning. However, neither have I assumed any gradual increase in this person's earnings over their lifetime and the straight line €45,900 average income assumption over the 40-year timeline is probably a significant understatement rather than an overstatement. But the principle is hopefully clear without getting bogged down in the maths.

Table 3.2: The Value of a 40-Year Savings Programme Starting at Age 26
Assuming 3% and 7% Annual Returns

Age	Investor A 3% return €	Investor B 7% return €
26	6,885	6,885
27	14,189	14,768
↓	↓	↓
65	519,792	1,381,233
Actual Invested	275,400	275,400
Investment Value	519,792	1,381,233
Growth (times)	1.9	5.0

Source: GillenMarkets.

Table 3.2 highlights a number of important points. Both investors saved a total of €275,400 over a 40-year period from age 26 to 65 inclusive. Investor A chose to save using bank deposits and grew her savings 1.9 times to €519,792 (before costs), while Investor B chose to invest in shares, and grew her savings 5.0 times to €1,381,233 (before costs). This is a theoretical and somewhat simplistic example as equity or stock market returns are never straight-line. Nonetheless, it highlights why – provided you can take a medium- to long-term view – one should seriously consider investing the majority of one's savings in risk assets like equities. If we assume risk-free bank deposits offer annual returns of 3% at age 65, Investor A would be able to generate a pre-tax annual return of €15,594 in retirement. Investor B, in contrast, would be generating a pre-tax income of €41,437 in retirement.

BUT TIME IS ALSO A POWERFUL FORCE IN COMPOUNDING

Table 3.3 highlights the situation of Investors C and D. It is a powerful example of compounding and demonstrates neatly why it's important to start a savings or investment programme, and particularly a pension savings programme, as early in life as you can. In fact, the earlier you start, the less capital you will need to commit to your programme.

Investor C starts to save the same €6,885 into her pension at age 26 and continues to add €6,885 to her investment programme each year until she is aged 40. That's 15 years of saving and a total investment of €103,275. She does not contribute anything further to her investment programme thereafter, but we'll assume she gets the long-term equity market returns of 7% *per annum* thereafter. She continues with her investment programme until she retires at age 65. At that point, her €103,275 of contributions is worth €945,763. She has multiplied her monies 9.2 times, without having added any new monies after age 40.

In contrast, Investor D starts her pension investment plan later in life at the age of 41, just when Investor C has finished contributing to her plan. However, Investor D contributes €6,885 into her investment programme each year for 25 years until she is aged 65 and gets the same annual return of 7% per annum. Over a period of 25 years, Investor D has put a total of €172,125 into her investment plan, substantially more than Investor C. At 65, her €172,125 is worth €437,914. She has multiplied her monies 2.5 times.

Table 3.3: The Comparison of a Savings Programme Started at Age 26 and Age 41

Age	Investor C Savings €	Value €	Investor D Savings €	Value €
26	6,885	7,367		
27	13,770	14,768		
28	20,665	22,686		
29	27,540	31,159		
↓	↓	↓		
40	103,275	174,256		
41		186,454	6,885	7,367
↓		↓	↓	↓
65		945,763	172,125	437,914
Total Invested		**103,275**		**172,125**
Return		**842,488**		**265,789**
Lump-sum at Retirement		**945,763**		**437,914**
Growth (times)		**9.2**		**2.5**

Source: GillenMarkets.

Since Investor C contributed just 60% of what Investor D contributed (€103,275 compared to €172,125), the interesting question is: How did Investor C end up with a larger lump-sum at retirement?

The answer is relatively straightforward. By the time Investor C stopped contributing to her investment programme at age 40, she had already compounded her savings to €174,256. She adds nothing further to her investment plan at this stage, but she continues to generate a 7% *per annum* return which, in her 41st year, is €12,198 and already well above the €6,885 that Investor D has just started to contribute to her pension savings plan. Investor D simply cannot catch up with Investor C in the time given. This is a striking example of the power of compounding, and of why time is a powerful force in compounding.

COMPOUNDING NEEDS TIME

At the age of 40, after 15 years of saving, Investor C had a lump-sum of €174,256. Of that €174,256, she had contributed €103,275, and the returns amounted to a smaller €70,981. Hence, in the first 15 years of her pension investment programme, it was more about what she had put into it than the returns she generated. However, over the subsequent 25 years, she contributed nothing further to her investment programme but generated returns of €771,507 (€945,763 less €174,256).

What this highlights, quite clearly, is that all the hard work is in the early years. In fact, for someone starting from scratch, compounding really doesn't start to kick in until about year seven or eight. It's over the initial couple of years that it feels like you are making little progress. But, once Investor C had an asset base built, compounding took over and it built momentum all on its own. No wonder Warren Buffett's biography was titled *Snowball!*[5] Build a snowball and start it rolling downhill; with momentum, it just keeps getting bigger and bigger all on its own. Likewise, in *Table 3.3*, Investor C's capital kept growing without any new contributions from her after age 40.

The key to financial freedom is to build an asset base from which you can generate an annual income that covers your overheads or outgoings.

---

[5]   Schroeder, A. (2008). *Snowball: Warren Buffett and the Business of Life*, New York: Bantam Books.

4: WAYS OF GAINING EXPOSURE TO MARKETS

As this booklet is addressing an Irish audience, there are two principal platforms through which the average person in Ireland can save and invest: the domestic life assurance industry and the global stock markets.

Figure 4.1: The Life Assurance Industry and the Stock Markets

Services	Life Assurance Industry	Stock Markets
Invest through	Intermediary	Stockbroker
Direct Share Investing	✗	✓
Fund Investing	✓	✓
Personal Savings	✓	✓
Pension Savings	✓	✓

THE LIFE INSURANCE INDUSTRY IN IRELAND

Through the domestic life assurance companies, you cannot invest directly in individual companies, government or corporate bonds. However, you can invest in funds that the life companies manage themselves or funds that they offer from third-party investment managers. Life company offerings typically include equity and property funds, bond funds, cash funds, guaranteed funds, hedge/absolute return funds and multi-asset funds. Each of the life companies in Ireland – which includes Aviva, Irish Life, New Ireland, Standard Life and Zurich – has a decent list of fund choices and fund solutions available. To invest in life company funds, be that for personal or pension savings, you normally have to go through an insurance broker, or life & pension broker.

The insurance broker assesses your risk profile, advises on a suitable fund or spread of funds and liaises directly with the life company regarding the purchase of a policy or plan. They also arrange for the transfer of your monies to the life company once appropriate application forms have been completed and money laundering documentation provided.

The fund type that life companies offer is typically a unit-linked fund, which is an open-ended fund. The term 'open-ended' means that when you invest in the unit-linked fund, the life company creates new units for you; when you redeem your investment, the life company cancels these units. In this way the unit price of the fund normally closely reflects the underlying value of the fund's investments.

In Ireland, there's no single platform for dealing in life company unit-linked funds so that, if you or your advisor wish to deal with several of the life companies, you will need to deal with each one separately. As we will soon see, this is a disadvantage when compared to the stockbroking platforms.

THE STOCK EXCHANGE PLATFORM

The stock market is the world's oldest investment platform – and it's global. By opening a stockbroking account, for personal or pension savings, you can invest directly into individual companies, exchange traded funds (ETFs) and investment trusts that are traded on any of the world's stock markets, as well as into a range of open-ended investment funds that increasingly can be accessed through stockbroking platforms. ETFs, investment trusts and investment funds provide investors with diversified exposure to all the major asset classes, including equities, government and corporate bonds, inflation-linked government bonds, precious metals, hedge/ absolute return funds, cash and currencies and a range of alternative assets.

Figure 4.2: Securities and Funds Accessible *via* Stockbroking Platforms

Security/Fund	Shares/Securities	Gross Roll-up Funds
Shares/Bonds	✓	
Exchange-traded Funds (ETFs)		✓
Investment Trusts	✓	
Investment Funds		✓

Shares, bonds, ETFs and investment trusts (which include REITs – Real Estate Investment Trusts) that are traded on stock exchanges are bought and sold through a stockbroker, either online or over the phone, by transacting with another investor in the marketplace. In the case of ETFs and investment trusts, which are in essence funds, the distinction here is that you do not deal with the asset management company (either directly or indirectly) that manages the fund. Dealing in shares, bonds, ETFs and investment trusts is continuous through the day until the market closes.

In contrast, to buy into (or invest in) open-ended investment funds, your monies are transferred by the stockbroker to the fund management company and they create new units for you in the fund, and these units are then reflected in your stockbroking account. Dealing in such funds is normally done at the end of each day or week. This is similar to how you invest in or redeem from a life company unit-linked fund.

It should be clear, then, that an investor has access to a much greater variety of investments through a stockbroking account, and can hold many different stocks and funds with no additional administration required for each separate purchase or sale.

In terms of supporting advice, you have a number of choices. If you opt for a traditional full-service advisory account, you can get advice from the stockbroking company you are with or have them manage monies for you on a discretionary basis (where they make the investment decisions). You can also appoint an independent financial advisory firm to provide you with advice and they will execute your orders for you on the stockbroking platform. If you are a confident do-it-yourself investor, then online stockbroking accounts provide you with a low-cost alternative where you make your own decisions. And there is an investment newsletter industry which, for an annual subscription fee, provides independent investment advice in a variety of formats. The investment newsletter industry is a large one in the US. At the time of writing, the GillenMarkets subscription-based investment newsletter is the only one in existence in Ireland.

EXCHANGE-TRADED FUNDS

The defining characteristics of ETFs are that they are open-ended funds that passively replicate the performance of a particular index, commodity or currency, and are listed on a recognised stock exchange. As such, for retail investors, ETFs are bought and sold in the same way as shares and by transacting with other investors in the marketplace.

ETFs simply aim to track an index or market, which is referred to as 'passive investment', and, as a consequence, they are low-cost funds as no fund manager is required and only minimal marketing and distribution costs are incurred in the establishment of an ETF.

While an investor does no better than the market with an ETF, they do no worse either. For investors, ETFs are a flexible and efficient way to manage personal savings or pension monies across the major asset classes. There are ETFs for investing in global equities, property, bonds and alternative assets like private equity and hedge/absolute return strategies. In addition, there are similar ETFs for regional and single country coverage.

Similar to unit-linked funds, new shares in an ETF can be created to cater for new institutional investors and shares can be cancelled as such investors exit. In this way, the share price of an ETF also normally reflects the underlying value of the fund's portfolio – the net asset value.

INVESTMENT TRUSTS

Investment trusts (known in the US as closed-end funds) are the oldest type of fund in the world, having been first used in London in the 19th century to finance the development of railroads in Latin and North America. Since then, they have grown to provide access to every asset class and most of the world's markets.

Investment trusts also offer an easy, cost-effective and risk-controlled method of managing your savings and pension monies in stock markets, and they, too, cover all the asset classes. In contrast to ETFs, investment trusts are actively-managed and therefore they are not as cheap as ETFs. There are numerous investment trusts or closed-ended funds listed on the US stock markets and over 300 listed on the London Stock Exchange.

REITs are a type of investment trust that invests in property. In Ireland, at the time of writing, there is just one REIT listed on the Irish Stock Exchange, Irish Residential REIT. This is down from four REITs a few years ago, as three of the REITs were taken over at a premium to the existing share price.

Again, to invest in an investment trust, the investor must transact with another investor in the marketplace similar to how you might buy shares in CRH, Kingspan or Kerry.

In contrast to open-ended investment funds or Irish unit-linked funds, an investment trust is a limited company and the amount of money the manager of an investment trust has to manage is fixed at the outset when the company raises its capital and lists onto the stock market. New shares are not routinely issued to satisfy the demand from new investors.

Demand and supply between investors in the marketplace is the main determinant of the share price of an investment trust. As a consequence, an investment trust's share price may diverge from the underlying value of its portfolio of investments – its net asset value or NAV. In the short-term, there can be imbalances between demand and supply, leading to a share price that is either above or below the value of the trust's NAV. In other words, the share price of an investment trust can trade at a premium or discount to the value of its portfolio.

Chart 4.1 highlights Irish Residential (IRES) REIT's share price and net asset value. The share price reflects the price at which buyers and sellers transact in Irish Residential REIT's shares in the marketplace, whereas Irish Residential REIT's net asset value reflects the underlying value of its portfolio of 4,000 mainly Dublin-based apartments as judged by professional auctioneers based on physical property transactions in the Irish residential property market.

Chart 4.1: Irish Residential REIT's Share Price & Net Asset Value

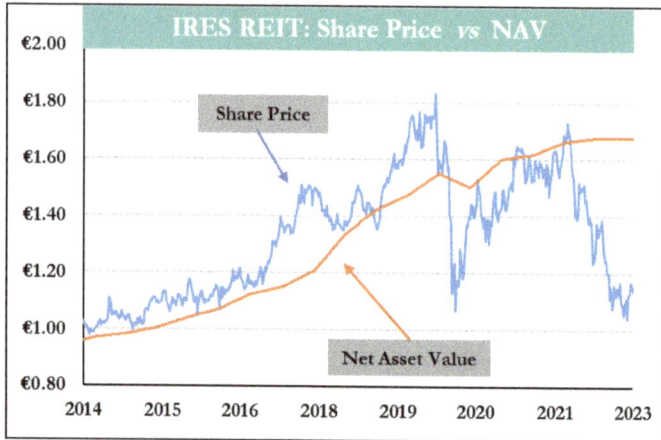

Source: Bloomberg and GillenMarkets.

As C*hart 4.1* highlights, Irish Residential REIT's share price traded at a premium to the value of its underlying property portfolio since it listed on the Irish Stock Exchange in 2014 up to 2019. In property downturns, however, it is common for the share prices of property REITs to decline below their net asset values. At the time of writing in early 2023, the Irish Residential REIT's share price is trading at a 31% discount to its net asset value. Why investor's currently place such a large discount on the value of IRES REIT's assets is something we address in our weekly investment newsletter for subscribers.

INVESTMENT FUNDS

Investment funds provide further choice and access to domestic and international fund managers. In the main they are actively managed funds, where a manager makes active investment decisions to invest in companies rather than simply copying the relevant stock market index. A benefit of an open-ended fund structure is that investors can regularly redeem and purchase shares in the fund at the net asset value of the fund. On the other hand, as investors have the choice to redeem units when they wish to, investment funds may not always be appropriate for more illiquid investments such as property or private equity. This contrasts with actively managed closed-end funds (investment trusts), where these funds raise capital when they initially list on the stock markets and while investors may trade shares amongst themselves, it does not reduce the investment capital available for the managers to invest. Accordingly, managers of investment trusts do not need to sell their underlying investments to meet investors' redemption needs, which may come at inappropriate times. For this reason, investment trusts are often more appropriate vehicles for investments that require longer term horizons such as property and private equity. Investors can still sell their positions, but they do so by selling their shares to other investors in the marketplace. And this does not harm the remaining investors.

Lastly, ongoing costs are generally higher with open-ended investment funds – compared to either ETFs or investment trusts – as the ongoing marketing and distribution efforts associated with continuously looking for new investors adds to costs.

TAXATION

For investors resident in Ireland, the taxation of shares and funds varies but, at the time of writing, the following is my understanding.

- **Shares, REITs and General Investment Trusts:** Dividends from shares are taxed as income at the investor's marginal rate of tax. Gains are taxed at the capital gains tax rate, currently 33%. Losses on shares can be offset against gains and unused losses can be carried forward indefinitely. The treatment of REITs is similar to shares as they are to all intents and purposes the same as shares. As general overseas investment trusts are not actually defined or dealt with in the Irish Revenue's legislation, it's not possible to be definitive on their tax treatment. That said, as general investment trusts are much the same as REITs, it is most likely that they should be taxed as shares and REITs.

- **Life Company Unit-linked Funds and Investment Funds:** Gains are currently taxed at 41% and there is no loss relief (losses cannot be

offset against gains), unless the funds are in the same umbrella
platform.

- **Exchange-traded Funds:** Only EU-domiciled ETFs are available to
  retail investors in Ireland, unless you have your assets managed by a
  professional investor on a discretionary basis, in which case you can
  access non-EU-domiciled ETFs. ETFs are generally established as
  Undertakings for Collective Investment in Transferable Securities
  (UCITS) and therefore taxed as gross roll-up funds, and gains and
  income are taxed at 41% and losses cannot be offset against gains.

5: DEFINING THE RISKS THAT INVESTORS FACE

The critical risks investors face are the risks that can lead to the permanent loss of capital. This definition of risk was introduced by Ben Graham in his book *The Intelligent Investor*, first published in 1949.[6] Fully understanding what risks can lead to a permanent loss of capital, how you can control them, and therefore how you can avoid them, enables you to become more comfortable with risk assets and a better investor. In my view, the principal risks are:

- The economic-specific risks;
- The asset-specific risks; and
- Speculating instead of investing.

THE ECONOMIC RISKS

The economy is generally in one of four states:

- Prosperity;
- Recession;
- Inflation; or
- Deflation.

Equities and property need economic prosperity to deliver returns. Fortunately, economic prosperity has been the norm over the decades, in the developed world at least. In Ireland, for example, living standards today are a multiple of what they were in, say, the 1940s. In a democratic and pro-business

---

6   Graham, B. (1973 [1949]). *The Intelligent Investor*, 4th Edition, New York: Harper & Row.

economy, things generally get better over time as people work and use their ingenuity to improve their lot.

Chart 5.1: The Economic Risks and Asset Types

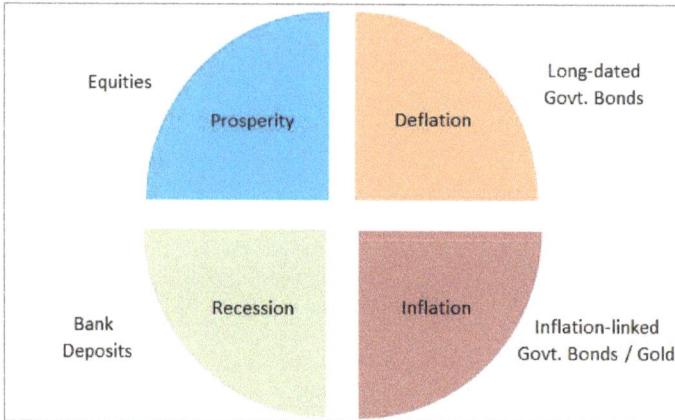

Recessions and inflation tend to hurt equities and property in the short-term, as they erode business earnings and property rental income. But this simply reflects the business cycle, and rarely leads to a permanent loss of capital. In other words, it has been right in the past to invest in equities and property.

Bank deposits are good to have when recessions hit, often because interest rates are normally rising prior to a recession to cool an overheating economy. Indeed, interest rates are often rising to cool inflation, so that bank deposits can be a decent asset either leading up to recessions or during periods of high inflation. In short, bank deposits can offer decent returns without risk in situations where equities and property returns are suffering.

Inflation-linked government bonds were introduced in the early 1980s and, in their simplest form, they come with a coupon (an interest rate), a guarantee of your capital back when the bond matures plus additional payments for unexpected inflation over the life of the bond. They offer an effective way to protect your assets against inflation over short- to medium-term horizons.

That said, good quality companies (shares), particularly those with pricing power, almost always recover from recessions, and adjust for inflation over time by raising their prices and repairing their margins. Property prices are not as vulnerable in recessions, unless they were overvalued at the outset, largely because the rental income that underpins property prices is, in the main, more stable than general business earnings. Property prices also tend to adjust for inflation over time. After all, if the costs of building a property rise due to inflation, existing properties will be more valuable and will also tend to keep up in value with inflation.

My point is that protecting yourself from the temporary losses that recessions and inflationary periods inflict on shares and property – by investing in non-risk assets that are less sensitive to the economy (like bank deposits, long-dated government bonds and inflation-linked government bonds) – is a choice and not always a necessity: such corrections mostly lead to temporary declines in stock market and property values, and rarely lead to a permanent loss of capital.

Deflation – the continual contraction of economic activity over a sustained period – on the other hand, is the mortal enemy of equities and property, as deflation in an economy can result in negative returns from equities and property assets over an extended period. Japan is a modern-day example of an economy that was mired in deflation for many years, which led to significant and persistent declines in both local share and property prices.

Fixed income government bonds, which provide a guarantee of your capital back after a set period of time and a pre-agreed income return over the same period, offer protection against deflation, as they did in Japan through its deflationary years of 1992 to 2012. After all, if you have a guarantee that your capital will be returned and that you'll be paid a set income, it doesn't really matter to you what state the economy is in over that period. Bank deposits or short-dated government bonds similarly provide a guarantee of your capital, but not of the income. The interest rate on bank deposits varies, and in a deflationary environment bank deposits rates will tend to decline substantially.

As we can't predict what state the economy is likely to be in with any accuracy or consistency, spreading your investments across the four major asset types outlined above – three of which are not sensitive to the economy and are generally labelled as non-risk assets (bank deposits, long-dated government bonds and inflation-linked government bonds) – can allow an investor to mitigate the economic risks outlined above.

But, as the global economy has tended to prosper over the long-term, which has favoured shares and property, spreading monies across the asset classes like this is a choice to be made rather than a necessity. As equities offer the best potential returns – on the assumption that they are not overvalued at the outset – an investor who spreads monies across the different asset classes should expect a lower return over time than is possible from equities and property. In **Chapter 6: MITIGATING THE RISKS**, we will see the actual returns for an investor who spread her savings or pension monies across the different asset classes over the 28-year period from 1995 to 2022.

Buying equities does not guarantee a good outcome, even when equities in general perform well, if an investor does not control the stock-specific risks. That said, if you invest in shares and property using funds, you can easily mitigate the stock-specific risks outlined below. So, controlling the risk of a permanent loss of capital inherent in owning shares can be achieved by:

- Diversifying across the four main asset classes; and/or
- Using fund structures to own shares.

The following section on stock-specific risks, therefore, is an optional read. If you don't intend to own individual shares, but rather to gain your exposure to equities through funds, just skip forward to the section on 'Speculating Instead of Investing' further on in this chapter.

STOCK-SPECIFIC RISKS

When it comes to businesses or companies, be they privately-owned or publicly-traded companies, the following three risks probably best describe what can lead to a permanent loss of capital:

- Business risks,
- Financial risks, and
- Valuation risks.

Control these three company-specific risks and you are most unlikely to suffer a permanent loss of capital when investing directly in shares.

Business Risks

These are the risks that the company will not be earning the same profits in five to 10 years' time as it is earning today. This risk is particularly hard to judge. It demands an understanding of different industries and many other business attributes.

Business models change and a good business model in one era is not necessarily a good business model in all economic and business conditions. Many business models are undermined by ongoing advances in technology. The travel agency; the newspaper industry; the bookseller; film, DVD and music distributors; and the traditional stockbroking industry, to name but a few, have all felt the impact of fresh challenges and new competition from advances in technology.

Changes in fashion occur at regular intervals in all areas of life, altering consumer habits, tastes and demand. The retail industry is in a constant state of flux, and companies in the sector that fail to adapt simply disappear, while new companies take their place with new products to satisfy the demands of the marketplace.

The regulations and legislation that drive many industries also change the landscape by creating opportunities and threats for both existing players and new entrants. For example, pharmaceutical companies are under constant threat of product patent expiry, which significantly reduces the margin on existing products, as new entrants are free to compete with the introduction of generic alternatives.

For these and many other reasons, the concept of a blue-chip stock, one that can be held for the long-term, is probably a misleading one. The simple fact is that there are far fewer true blue-chip stocks in the global markets than most investors appreciate.

Financial Risks

These are the risks that the company has inappropriate financing or debt levels that can undermine shareholder value. If a company has too much debt and breaches its banking agreements (covenants), then shareholder equity can be imperilled. Again, this risk is not easy for non-professional investors to assess, as different industries can accommodate different levels of debt for a given cash flow stream.

We need look no further than the Irish banks for a classic example of financial risk. Following the introduction of the euro in 1999, Irish banks were able to access credit from European banks without any increase in the cost of that credit (to reflect the increasing economic risks in Ireland of an overheating economy). The Irish banks lent on this credit to builders and property developers. But the funds were mostly lent against grossly overvalued property assets. When the developers and builders could not repay, shareholders in banks were wiped out. But for the State guarantee, bond holders, and quite possibly depositors also, would have suffered considerable losses.

Valuation Risks

These are the risks of overpaying, even for a good company, to the extent that you compromise the long-term returns available from the shares in that company.

Chart 5.2: Coca-Cola's Share Price and Earnings per share (1988 – 2022)

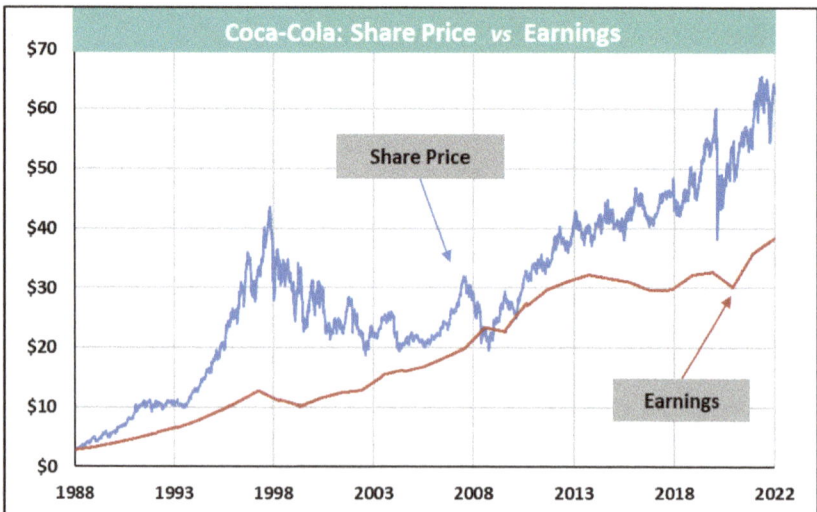

Source: Bloomberg, Coca Cola Annual Reports and GillenMarkets.

Chart 5.2 highlights Coca-Cola's share price and earnings (with the earnings series rebased to the share price back in late 1988 for ease of comparison). It can be readily seen from the chart that Coca-Cola's share price did not surpass the peak of mid-1998 until 2016, some 18 years later. In other words, over the intervening 18 years from 1998 to 2016, an investor who bought Coca-Cola's shares in mid-1998 saw no capital growth. Yes, an investor received the annual dividend, but little else. At the time of writing, Coca-Cola's share price is, once again, a long way ahead of the underlying earnings trend. However, today's share price is just 50% above the earnings trend. Back in 1998, Coca-Cola's share price was 300% the earnings trend.

The problem back in 1998 was not Coca-Cola's earnings, as management grew earnings from *circa* $0.75 a share in mid-1998 to $1.91 a share by 2016. No, the chief problem in mid-1998 was investors overpaying for the shares relative to the company's underlying earnings and growth potential at the time. This can also be clearly seen in **Chart 5.2** where we can see the huge divergence of the share price from earnings back in the mid- to late-1990s.

If you can't identify these company-specific risks – and few private investors can – then investing through funds is a viable alternative. Diversification through funds covers both the business and financial risks. It does not, however, cover valuation risk. After all, it is possible for an entire market to be overvalued. Hence, the ability to value equities or property in general is also important but is beyond the scope of this booklet.

VOLATILITY IN MARKETS IS NOT THE ENEMY

If the above represents a fair description of what investment risk in a specific company (share) is, then volatility in equity markets and individual shares can be understood for what it really is: not risk as such – unless you need your capital back in the near-term – but the expression of investors' fears. In that regard, lower markets that offer better values should be welcomed by the investor who, on such occasions, has the understanding and flexibility to add monies to her investment programme.

On our 1-day investment training seminars, I have often explained why volatility in stock markets is not actually risk using an alternative analogy.

Say you own and run a private supermarket. Most likely the risks you face as a business are exactly the same as those faced by a Tesco or a Sainsbury, both of which are listed on the London Stock Exchange. Your risks are the business risks you face: product supply, changing customer preferences, new competitors setting up around the corner, etc., the financial risks of having taken on debt for new projects or store expansion and the valuation risks of possibly having bought the business off someone else at too high a price. Private companies face exactly the face risks as publicly-traded businesses. But they don't have a share price and the value of their business does not jump around daily. So, I think we can acknowledge that the risks faced by both entities are essentially the same, and as private companies don't have a share price or daily quote, this might help us to see that the volatility in the share price in and of itself is not actually risk. It may be investors' expressions of risk, or the proxy for risk, but it is not the actual risk itself.

If one of the above supermarkets has taken on too much debt and trading conditions deteriorate for the food retail sector as a whole, the indebted company faces increased financial risk. And, if that is the publicly-traded company, its share price may well start to reflect that. So, the declining share price is reflecting the increased risks associated with having taken on (possibly) too much debt.

SUCCESSFUL INVESTING IS NOT ABOUT FORECASTING

Once you understand what the risks actually are, and how you can mitigate or control them, then making a success out of investing does not require you to be Einstein nor does it require you to forecast anything. You are, however, required to decide whether your glass is half-full or half-empty. And, in that regard, each of us is different.

A good investment plan requires you to decide at the outset what risks you wish to avoid and to invest in assets that avoid those risks. For example, if you believe that deflation is a high risk globally, then you have little choice but to invest in assets that are unaffected by deflation (for example, bank deposits and long-dated government bonds), assuming they are not overvalued. This is an issue I will return to in **Chapter 7: IMPLEMENTING A PLAN**.

GUARANTEED PRODUCTS ARE NOT THE ANSWER

Investment products that provide a guarantee on your capital (80%, 90% or even a 100% guarantee) proliferate in Ireland, so many readers may think that investing in these simple-sounding products is the way to mitigate the risks. It is not!

The Global Financial Crisis led to pain for both equity and property investors, so the idea that you can invest in a risk-asset fund which offers the prospect of much higher returns than are available from bank deposits with limited downside, reflecting the guarantee, has significant attractions for both the investor and the advisor. However, in the majority of cases, the upside proves illusory because the high costs within guaranteed products weigh too heavily on the normal returns available from the underlying assets.

Another way of saying this is that the costs of making these products, distributing them, and paying for the insurance that provides the guarantee, normally eat too much into the returns that the underlying assets can provide. In short, guaranteed products largely reward the sellers, not the buyers.

SPECULATING INSTEAD OF INVESTING

Constant activity in markets is the hallmark of the trader or speculator. The primary role of stock markets is to match the financing needs of companies with the investment needs of savers, but because of the liquidity available in markets – where you can buy and sell almost instantaneously - the markets also fulfil the gambling instincts in human nature.

To be an investor is to be an owner of assets. By owning shares in businesses or properties, you are a part-owner of the underlying assets, and should benefit from the returns that these assets generate over time. All investors can earn these returns, just as they can, and have done, with physical property over time.

In contrast, the trader or speculator – who is attempting to buy low and sell high in markets over short time intervals – does not have the time to benefit from the underlying growth in the markets that occurs over longer periods. For this reason, the trader or speculator is playing a 'zero-sum game'. His gain must be someone else's loss. In fact, due to transaction costs (dealing costs, stamp duty, etc.), the trader or speculator is usually playing a negative-sum game.

The average house price in Ireland in 1970 was *circa* €7,000. Today, despite the calamity that befell Irish house prices between 2007 and 2012, the average house price as of 2022 is *circa* €359,000. If you owned the property over this period, you obtained the return. It's not a zero-sum game over the long-term.

As incomes in a prospering society grow, people can afford to pay a higher price for that same property. In 1970, the average income of those employed was *circa* €2,000. Today, it is *circa* €45,900. This rise in average incomes goes a long way to explaining why the average house price in Ireland is substantially higher today than in 1970. It works the same way with businesses listed on stock markets. As earnings of individual businesses rise, their value, and therefore their share prices, also rise over time.

Spread-betting accounts and Contracts-for-Difference accounts, which encourage you to trade markets and provide you with a borrowing facility if you want to borrow, should be avoided like the plague.

It's also worth remembering that, if you trade markets, you are up against the professional traders in investment banks and hedge funds. Amateur sportspeople do not expect to beat professional sportspeople, be that at tennis, squash, golf or any other sport. There's a temptation to believe that it's different in markets. It is not. Recognise that, if you try and trade markets, you are, in effect, gambling, and you might as well be down in the bookies.

6: MITIGATING THE RISKS

For the majority of non-professional investors, effective strategies for mitigating the risks of a permanent loss include diversifying (especially within equities), investing regularly over time, spreading your savings across risk assets as well as non-risk assets, and having some patience. Some or all of these strategies can greatly assist you to mitigate:

- The risks of investing in individual companies;
- The short-term volatility that is ever present in stock markets; and
- The economic risks of recession, inflation and deflation.

DIVERSIFYING IN SHARES IS MANDATORY

Regardless of whether you prefer to invest in individual companies or through funds, the following is a striking example of the need for diversification within equities. I introduced this particular message into the GillenMarkets 1-day investment training seminars in 2013 after a colleague of mine, Dermot Walsh of Davy, first articulated this method of presentation to me. There's no point in reinventing the wheel when it has been handed to you!

As we outlined in **Chapter 5: DEFINING THE RISKS THAT INVESTORS FACE**, the rationale for diversifying among individual shares or businesses is to avoid the business, financial and valuation risks that can lead to a permanent loss of capital.

Table 6.1 highlights the performance of a portfolio of just six shares from the peak in the Irish equity market on 1st February 2007 through to the close of business on 31st December 2015. The six shares in the portfolio have been selected from different industries, thus improving diversification further. All in all, it's a powerful demonstration of the benefits of basic diversification.

Table 6.1: The Benefits of Diversification in a Six-Stock Portfolio

Asset	Industry	Price Feb 2007 €	Dec 2015 €	Gain / Loss
Allied Irish Banks	Banking	5,675.00	6.66	-99.9%
CRH	Building Materials	28.31	26.83	-5.2%
DCC	Business Services	24.21	76.80	217.3%
Kerry	Food Ingredients	20.00	76.31	281.6%
Ryanair	Airline	5.61	15.01	167.6%
FBD	General Insurance	40.28	6.61	-83.6%
Average Share Price Gain				79.6%
Dividend Income				19.9%
Total Return				99.6%

Source: Bloomberg and GillenMarkets.

While AIB went bust, and effectively declined 100%, the performance of the overall portfolio is up 79%, or 99% if you include the dividend income you would have received from such a portfolio over the 2007 to 2015 period.

Owning the banks' shares in Ireland through the Irish banking and government fiscal crises was a catastrophe. However, had you spread your monies across just six different industries, you would have survived the worst stock market downturn since the mid-1930s.

Table 6.2 makes the same point in a perhaps more striking way. Owning just one stock, a bank, resulted in a 99.9% loss. There's no recovering from that.

Table 6.2: Progressive Gain / Loss in a Six-Stock Portfolio (2007 to 2015)

No. of holdings	2007-2015 Gain / Loss
1	-99.9%
2	-91.7%
3	-62.9%
4	+7.1%
5	+62.0%
6	+79.6%

Source: GillenMarkets.

By adding in a second stock, FBD Insurance, which was down 83% from 1st Feb 2007 to 31st December 2015, the combined holdings resulted in a loss of 91.7%. Adding in a third stock, CRH, reduced the portfolio loss to 62.9%. Adding in a fourth stock, DCC, swung the portfolio into profit with a gain of 7.1%. Adding in a fifth stock, Kerry, transformed the situation and lifted the overall portfolio to a gain of 62%. Adding in the sixth and final stock, Ryanair, lifted the average share price gain to 79.6%. As outlined above, dividend income improved the overall returns further to almost 100%.

Diversifying within shares can be done by owning a portfolio of at least 10 stocks spread across different industries and geographies. Funds also do an excellent job of diversifying an investor across many different companies, industries and geographic regions.

INVESTING REGULARLY COVERS A LOT OF RISKS

Even when you are diversified, you can still buy an overvalued asset, be that a property, a share or an entire market. The task of understanding when assets are overvalued is beyond the majority of private investors. Even professional investors find it hard to be definitive about when individual companies or entire markets are overvalued. However, investing regularly in good times and bad, in up and down markets, can assist the private investor to mitigate the risks of obtaining poor value at a single point in time.

To make the point, I'm going to use the example of an investor who decided to track the performance of the FTSE World (Equity) Index. **Chart 6.1** shows the price performance of the FTSE World Index from the start of 2000 to the end of 2022. At the start of 2000, there was no exchange-traded fund that an investor could buy to mirror the performance of the FTSE World Index. Today, there is a plethora of them.

So, **Chart 6.1** acts as a (very accurate) proxy for the journey an investor went on, if they choose to invest regularly in the FTSE World Index. At the time in early 2000, the developed equity markets were seriously overvalued, so that there was serious valuation risk in global equities at that time.

Chart 6.1: FTSE World Index (2000 to 2022)

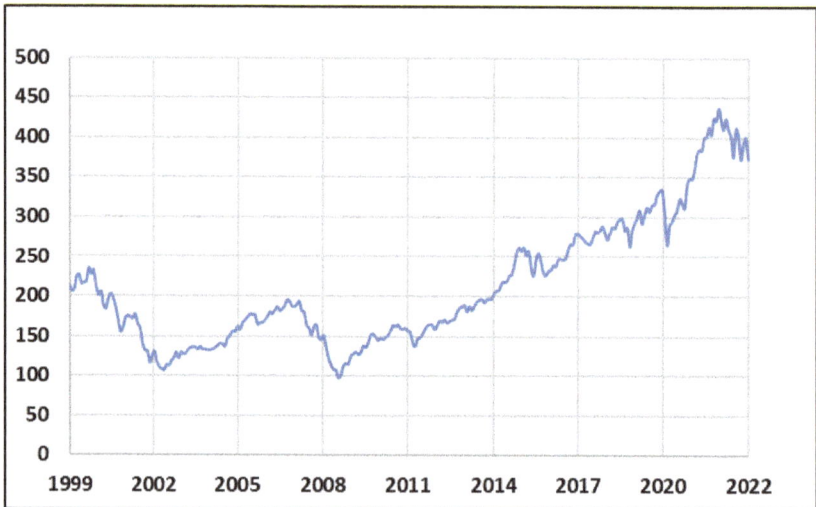

Source: Bloomberg

At the end of December 2022, the FTSE World Index was 76% ahead of the early January 2000 level. This represented a 2.5% compound *per annum* return, or a 4.9% compound *per annum* including dividends reinvested. These returns are well below historical norms and reflect the fact that the developed world equity markets were expensive compared to history back in late 1999.

For an investor who made a single investment into the World Equity Index (*via* an ETF or other fund type), the subsequent returns were both volatile and below average. However, for the regular investor, the outcome was entirely different.

In **Chapter 3: THE POWER OF COMPOUNDING**, we saw that saving 10% from an average income in Ireland into a pension account with a 5% top-up from your employer made for an annual savings programme of €6,885. Our next example in *Chart 6.2* assumes a monthly savings programme in the FTSE World Index of €500 per month, or €6,000 a year.

Chart 6.2 highlights the progress of such a monthly investment programme into the FTSE World Index starting on 1st January 2000 and ending on 31st December 2022.

Chart 6.2: Value of €500 Invested Monthly (less costs) in the FTSE World Index Starting on 1st January 2000 until 31st December 2022

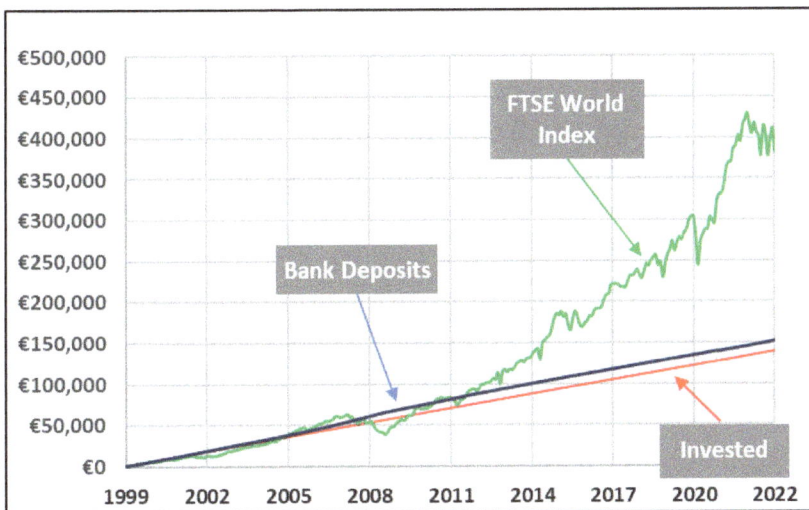

Source: GillenMarkets.

We will assume that the savings programme is in a pension account, so that there are no taxes to account for. We have assumed a 1.0% transaction cost on each monthly contribution.

At end December 2022, the regular investor's pension fund had invested a total of €138,500 (after costs) *via* monthly contributions. The value of those contributions had grown to €382,112. The investor's capital has grown 2.76

times. The positive outcome may surprise you when you consider **Chart 6.1** earlier, which highlighted that the FTSE World Index was up just 76% over that same timeline. There are three factors that explain the positive outcome:

- By committing to investing regularly, the investor was investing both when global equity markets were overvalued and undervalued;
- The investor obtained a dividend income stream from the index which was reinvested; and
- The investor benefitted from euro-cost averaging, a much underappreciated technique for taking advantage of lower prices in the stock markets.

Euro-cost Averaging

Because a regular investor invests the same amount of money each month (or at some other regular interval), she is able to buy more shares when prices are lower. For example, investing her monthly €500 in January 2000 at the then FTSE World Index price of 211.92 bought her 2.34 index shares. But in February 2009, following sharp falls in global stock markets during the global financial crisis, and with the FTSE World Index price at a much lower €96.90, the same €500 monthly commitment bought her a more significant 5.11 index shares. This is called dollar- or euro-cost averaging, and it works well over time. **Table 6.3** demonstrates this.

Table 6.3: An Example of Euro-cost Averaging in the FTSE World Index with a Monthly €500 Investment (January 2000 to December 2022)

Total Invested	€138,500
No. of Shares Bought	734
Weighted Average Price Achieved	€188.73
Average Share Price	€212.72
Difference	**11.3%**

Source: GillenMarkets.

Over the entire period, the average price of the FTSE World Index was €212.72. Yet, the investor invested a total of €138,500 and bought 734 index shares for a weighted average price of €188.73. So, despite the fact that the FTSE World

Index price was just 76% above where it was on 1st January 2000, by averaging in, the investor obtained a weighted average price that was 11.3% below the unweighted average price pertaining over the period. This, plus the dividend income, compounded her €138,500 investment to €383,112 for a satisfactory outcome.

Of course, **Chart 6.2** also highlights that while the investor started an investment programme in January 2000, the value of her investment was below the amount she had invested some eight years later in early 2009. The subsequent strong recovery in global equity markets from March 2009 onwards meant that her investment recovered rapidly thereafter and moved on to new highs. However, there's no hiding the fact that the 2000s were a difficult decade for investors, reflecting both the fact that the developed stock markets were overvalued at the outset and the impact of two recessions. Even regular investing could not overcome these conditions until into the 2010s. At such times, an investor needs patience.

Our example here has used the FTSE World Index because no exchange-traded fund (ETF) existed at that time to track the world index for investors. Today, there are a plethora of ETFs that can passively track the world index for you and at very low cost. In other words, the example we outline in this section is very realistic.

Lastly, **Chart 6.2** also highlights the very low returns from bank deposits in the Eurozone over the same period, emphasising again the benefits of buying equities as opposed to saving through the lower-risk bank deposits.

THE BENEFITS OF DIVERSIFYING ACROSS ASSET CLASSES

The regular investing example works well if an investor is investing over a lifetime and has the time to wait for recovery along the way. But it does not work for investors who have neither the time to wait for recovery nor the flexibility to add to their investment programme when prices are lower (and values better).

As we discussed in **Chapter 5: DEFINING THE RISKS THAT INVESTORS FACE**, lump-sum investors – who can't afford to be at the mercy of the economy, or who haven't the time to wait for recovery – can diversify into risk assets and non-risk assets alike which, in combination, normally offer inflation-plus returns over time, and which also offset the risks of recession, inflation and deflation.

Chart 6.3 highlights the returns profile for a lump-sum investor who invested her savings equally into the five major asset classes (equities, long-dated government bonds, inflation-linked government bonds, bank deposits and gold) at the start of 1995. The portfolio is rebalanced annually to ensure a constant 20% allocation to each asset type. In a pension structure, there are no tax implications of making the necessary annual changes. Outside a pension structure, tax complications can be overcome by investing across the asset classes like this through a fund structure, as changes made within a fund are not taxed within the fund.

Chart 6.3: The Value of €10,000 Invested equally between Equities, Long-dated Government Bonds, Inflation-linked Government Bonds, Bank Deposits & Gold (1995 to 2022)

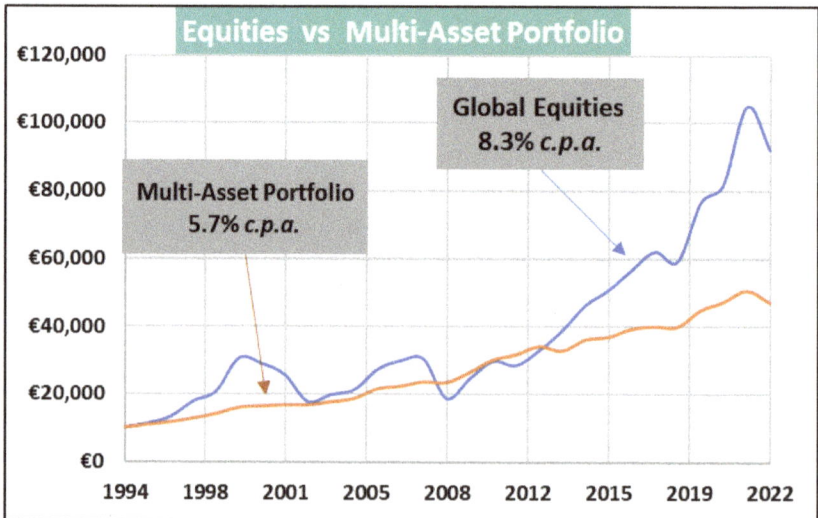

Source: Bloomberg and GillenMarkets.

Chart 6.3 highlights that, from the start of 1995 to end 2022, investing a €10,000 lump-sum equally across the five asset classes delivered an annual return of 5.7% (ignoring costs, for the sake of simplicity), and turning the

€10,000 investment into €47,153 over this 28-year timeline. Eurozone bank deposit interest rates averaged *circa* 1.8% and inflation averaged *circa* 2.1% over the same 28-year period.

The chart also highlights that the volatility in such a portfolio was low: the portfolio suffered an annual loss in just four years out of 28, with the worst loss at 6.9% in 2022.

So, for those investors who:

- Can't afford to be at the mercy of the economy;
- Don't like volatility;
- Can't take advantage of lower prices and the better values they bring; or
- Don't have the time to wait for recovery

allocating savings or pension monies across the five major asset classes – to both non-risk assets and risk assets – has, in the past, assisted in mitigating the major economic risks while still offering the potential for inflation-plus returns.

LUMP-SUM INVESTING IN EQUITIES NEEDS A FIVE-YEAR PLUS TIME HORIZON

With lump-sum investing in particular, if you are investing in risk assets like shares and/or property, it is best to take a five-year plus view at least. Taking a five-year plus view normally allows time for stock markets to recover from the effects of economic recession and avoids the scenario where an investor panics in response to a downturn and sells out in anticipation of further declines. Often, selling at such times occurs when everyone else is selling and can lead to a permanent loss when none needs to be taken.

Over the long-term, our examination of US stock market returns since 1926 highlights that the probability of generating a positive return from global stock markets over the following timelines is as follows:

- 76% over a five-year view;
- 90% over a 10-year view; and
- 99% over a 20-year view.

In other words, a well-diversified share portfolio, especially one offering reasonable value, has a high probability of positive returns once a medium- to long-term view is taken.

For investors who can add to their personal savings or pension assets over time and who take advantage of lower prices and the often better values that they offer, the probability of positive returns on a five- to 10-year timeline increases significantly further. In fact, it has been quite rare for an investor who is investing regularly over time to suffer a loss on a five-year view.

7: IMPLEMENTING A PLAN

KEY DECISIONS

The first issue to sort out is whether, within equities, you are prepared to invest in individual shares or whether you are more comfortable using funds. For many private investors, it is easier to use funds and the modest extra annual cost involved is probably well worth it for the risks avoided.

The second, and more important, issue to sort out is whether you are a regular investor or a lump-sum investor.

A STRATEGY FOR THE REGULAR INVESTOR

We define a regular investor as one who either doesn't have a lump-sum to invest at the outset or, if she does, it's not large in relation to the monies she can add to her investment programme over time (be that a personal savings or pension programme). The regular investor is investing over time, in rising and falling markets, so that as we saw in **Chapter 6: MITIGATING THE RISKS**, the risk of mistiming her entry into equity markets is much reduced. Hence, I feel that most regular investors who plan to be saving and investing over the long-term can take higher risks and invest exclusively in shares (equities), where the returns have been highest over the long-term.

Investing exclusively in equities requires a glass-half-full attitude. While history is on the side of equities, we can never tell what the future holds, so there is a risk that equities or property won't work out. Of course, there's nothing wrong with not committing all your savings to risk assets like shares or property. To each her own!

This booklet can't address each reader individually, but if you keep things simple you can invest successfully in less than an hour a year. For exposure to equities, if you don't know what shares to buy or don't know which country or sectors offer the best value, why not just invest in a global equity fund? Passively managed global exchange-traded funds (ETFs), actively managed global equity investment trusts and funds, or global equity unit-linked funds from one of the domestic life companies will all do the job.

Table 7.1: Selected Global Equity Funds

	Ticker	Market	Currency
Exchange-traded Funds			
db X-Trackers MSCI World	XDWD GY	Germany	€
Vanguard FTSE All-World	VWRL NA	Netherlands	€
Investment Trusts			
Murray International	MYI LN	London	£
Bankers Trust	BNKR LN	London	£
JP Morgan Global G & I	JGGI LN	London	£
Smithson Investment Trust	SSON LN	London	£
Investment Funds			
FundSmith Equity Fund	n/a	n/a	€
2Xideas Global Mid-cap Fund	n/a	n/a	€
Unit-linked Funds			
Zurich Dividend Growth Fund	n/a	n/a	€

Source: GillenMarkets.

Note: Investment Trusts listed in Table 7.1 are taxed as shares, so that gains are taxed at the capital gains tax rate (33%), dividend income at your marginal rate and losses can be offset against gains. ETFs, Investment Funds and Unit-Linked Funds are gross roll-up funds and, outside a pension structure, gains are taxed at 41% and there's no loss relief available.

Table 7.1 provides you with a small selection of low-cost, passively managed global ETFs, as well as actively managed global equity investment trusts, global investment funds and a global unit-linked fund from Zurich (Ireland). The ETFs and investment trusts can be bought through traditional and online stockbrokers just like any share. These days, most online stockbroking platforms also facilitate the purchase and sale of investment funds. Both of the investment funds we outline in **Table 7.1** can be accessed *via* the Davy Select platform in Dublin. You can buy units in the unit-linked fund through intermediaries or insurance brokers.

By investing in one or more of these funds regularly over time you should achieve better returns than bank deposits over the medium- to long-term, as has been the case in the past. The list of funds is by no means exhaustive. While the investment trusts are quoted in sterling, this does not mean you are exposed to sterling exclusively. Each fund is diversified globally so that, in reality, you have a spread of currency exposure in all of them.

A STRATEGY FOR THE LUMP-SUM INVESTOR

If you have a lump-sum to invest and are unlikely to be in a position to add meaningfully to that lump-sum over time, I would describe you as a lump-sum investor.

As a lump-sum investor, you can still choose to invest exclusively in shares and property assets, so long as you understand that you need to be able to assess the value you are buying and, ideally, be in a position to invest for a five- to 10-year period, at least.

Clearly, the risks of mistiming your entry into markets and overpaying for shares or property assets are higher for the lump-sum investor. If you wish to mitigate these and other risks as outlined in **Chapter 6: MITIGATING THE RISKS**, you have the choice of allocating your monies across the different asset classes – to invest in both risk assets and non-risk assets.

But, as I noted at the end of that chapter, an investor who wishes to minimise risk in their portfolio has to accept that the returns normally will be lower than those available from equities.

Table 7.2 provides you with a selection of funds that are listed on stock markets, and which can be bought into a stockbroking account to build a portfolio of assets balanced between risk and non-risk assets. Again, this list is not exhaustive and there are many alternative securities and funds that fit the bill. The table also includes two funds that invest across the asset classes (multi-asset or balanced funds) and, while they are not listed funds, but investment funds, they are, nonetheless, available *via* the Davy Select online platform in Ireland.

Table 7.2: Selected Funds for Investing in Equities, Long-dated Govt. Bonds, Short-dated Govt. Bonds, Inflation-linked Govt. Bonds & Gold

	Reference	Fund Type	Market	Currency
Equities				
Vanguard Total World ETF	VWRL NA	ETF	US	€
Bankers Trust	BNKR LN	Inv. Trust	London	£
Long-dated Government Bonds				
iShares € Govt. Bond (10-15 years)	EUN8 GY	ETF	Germany	€
Short-dated Government Bonds				
iShares € Govt. Bond (1-3 years)	CSBGE3 SW	ETF	Swiss Exchange	€
Inflation-linked Bonds				
iShares € Inflation-Linked Govt. Bond	IBCI GY	ETF	Germany	€
Gold Exchange-traded Commodity				
iShares Physical Gold ETC	SGLN LN	ETC	London	$
Mixed Asset Funds				
Ruffer Total Return International Fund	n/a	Inv. Fund	UK	€
Trojan Fund	n/a	Inv. Fund	Dublin	€

Source: Bloomberg & GillenMarkets.

OPENING A STOCKBROKING ACCOUNT – SAVINGS & PENSION MONIES

If you are interested in saving and investing through the stock markets, you will need to open a personal and/or pension stockbroking account, if you don't already have one. Your main choice is between a traditional broker and an online broker. Irish stockbrokers tend to have a dual offering and you can choose whichever offering suits you. A traditional broker provides a fuller service and mainly takes orders by phone or email, and provides execution-only, advisory and discretionary fund management services. Understandably, the cost of transacting through traditional stockbrokers for private investors is higher than through online brokers.

Security of Client Assets

The same regulations apply to all stockbrokers in regard to the security of client assets. For that reason, your assets are as secure with online brokers as they are with traditional brokers. The broker must hold your cash balances through local banks, and shares and bonds bought on your behalf must be held by a third-party global custodian. These measures ensure, as far as they can, segregation of duties and that your assets remain safe in the event that the stockbroker itself gets into financial difficulty.

A Path to Financial Freedom

Learning how to save and invest is not a luxury, it is a crucial part of our lives, and if you want to achieve financial freedom, you need to be more informed. That we learn little about even the basics of saving and investing in school or university is part of the problem.

Written by Rory Gillen, founder of GillenMarkets and author of *3 Steps to Investment Success*, published in 2012, this booklet outlines why the stock markets and property have delivered the best returns over the long-term, how to define and mitigate the major economic risks and the difference between investing and speculating. It also makes a crucial distinction between the risks faced by the regular investor and the lump-sum investor, outlines a sound investment plan for each and shows you how to get started.

Gillen.

E: info@gillenmarkets.com
T: +353 1 2871400
W: www.gillenmarkets.com